HOSPITALITY

Allan Havis

BROADWAY PLAY PUBLISHING INC
New York
www.broadwayplaypublishing.com
info@broadwayplaypublishing.com

First published by B P P I in July 1989 in the collection *Plays By Allan Havis*
First printing this edition: September 2011
I S B N: 978-0-88145-503-8

Book design: Marie Donovan
Page make-up: Adobe Indesign
Typeface: Palatino
Printed and bound in the U S A

ABOUT THE AUTHOR

The plays of Allan Havis have produced by San Diego Rep, Old Globe/Malashock Dance, Vox Nova, Seattle's A C T, Odyssey, Long Wharf, South Coast Rep, American Repertory Theater, Hartford Stage, Virginia Stage, W P A, Berkshire Theater Festival, Trapdoor Theater, Coral Gable's New Theater, Interact Theater, Philadelphia Theater Co, K P B S Radio, Vox Nova, and Rowholt Theater-Verlag (National German Radio). Commissions from San Diego Rep, England's Chichester Festival, Sundance, San Diego Rep, Ted Danson's Anasazi Productions, South Coast Rep, Mixed Blood, C S C Rep, Malashock Dance, Carolina Chamber Chorale, National Foundation for Jewish Culture, and University of California. Fifteen full length published plays, and also a Harper & Row novel *Albert the Astronomer*. He has edited two anthologies: *American Political Plays* (2001) University of Illinois Press and *American Political Plays After 9/11* (2010) Southern Illinois University Press. Also, his book on ninety years of cult cinema, *Cult Films: Taboo & Transgression*, (2008) University Press of America. In collaboration with renowned composer Anthony Davis, his play *Lilith* was re-imagined as an opera, premiered at U C San Diego's Conrad Prebys Concert Hall December 2009 and broadcasted on U C S D T V in 2010. Recipient of Guggenheim, Rockefeller, Kennedy Center/American Express, C B S, H B O,

National Endowment for the Arts Awards, San Diego Theater Critics Circle 2003 Outstanding New Play for NUEVO CALIFORNIA (co-written with Bernardo Solano) and San Diego's 2008 Patté Best Play award for THE TUTOR. He earned an M F A from Yale. He is provost of Thurgood Marshall College/University of California, San Diego and a professor of Theater in the M F A program.

HOSPITALITY was first produced by the Philadelphia Theater Company in April 1988. The cast and creative contributor were:

HAPPY...Larry Pine
FULLER... Herb Downer
CORTEZ ....Patricia Mauceri
AGUNEIR... Ronald Hunter
MONTEITH...Robert Trumbull

Director... William Foeller

The play was subsequently produced in London by North American Theater at the Viceroy Pub in January and February 1989. The cast were:

HAPPY..Stephen Hoye
FULLER.. Neville Aurelius
CORTEZ .... Lesley Joseph
AGUNEIR.. Norman Chancer
MONTEITH ....Ed Bishop

CHARACTERS & SETTING

HAPPY, *male, 40s, white, Immigration Agent*
FULLER, *male, 40s, black, Immigration Agent*
CORTEZ, *female, 30s, Spanish journalist/Colombia*
AGUNEIR, *male, 50s, Israeli politician*
MONTEITH, *male, 50s, white, Immigration Supervisor from Washington*

A detention center in New York City. The rooms are ascetic and bare. There is a lounge for the agents and conference room.

The time is 1986.

Scene One

(Day One. CORTEZ's *Room)*

HAPPY: Let's not fool ourselves...a vegetarian lives longer, has finer bowel movements, and maintains a superior memory. You keep friends, have better breath, and lend an undeniable kindness to the animal kingdom. I read this in a clinic in Geneva when I detoxed. Raw or cooked, you're better off this way. When I glanced at your files, I was glad to recognize an ally in the kitchen. Miss Cortez, I am your ally. And your secret admirer. *(Pause)* You're a very attractive woman, if I may say. Are you hungry?

CORTEZ: No.

HAPPY: Thirsty? *(Pause)* I trust you're comfortable? Room service, cable T V, a wet bar, kleenexes, just like a hotel... Efficiently run. In a day or two, you may wish to dine downstairs in the commons. That's where we all eat. It's more social that way. Better for one's psychology. *(Pause)* They've assigned me to you. Frankly, it's quite an honor. You're a renowned poet and author. A playwright and actor. An inspired leader to our people. I hope I won't be a nuisance, Miss Cortez. I'm here to sort out the mess. *(Pause)* I was supposed to read your works yesterday, but my wife had chores for me. Still, my assistants have perused them, in Spanish and English...their notes are disturbing. You don't rhyme, Miss Cortez. You use vulgar images for comic affect. And your literature insults men. American men. Well, I won't fault you for that. I really can't. Poetic license.

CORTEZ: I'm not a poet. I am a journalist.

HAPPY: What?

CORTEZ: Idiot. You mistake me for someone else.

HAPPY: Your name is Cortez? Sophia Margarite Cortez?

CORTEZ: Yes.

HAPPY: But you're not the Peruvian poet and actor?

CORTEZ: I am a Colombian journalist. Read your files.

HAPPY: How can this be? It says in my report...

CORTEZ: I'm here by invitation of Harvard University. My papers are in order. You have my passport and visa. I cannot protest enough about this infringement.

HAPPY: We've a new girl on staff, Miss Cortez, and perhaps some papers were shuffled. Perhaps we've confused you with Angelica Cordoba?

CORTEZ: I think you have.

HAPPY: Yes, yes. Cordoba writes plays. You write hoary leftist essays. It says so right here. Well, well, I must look like a horse's ass. Shall we start over again? *(Broad smile)* My name is Happy. Agent Logan. We like first names at Immigration. Relax, Miss Cortez. A vegetarian lives longer, has finer bowel movements, and maintains a superior memory. Raw or cooked, you're better off this way. You are a vegetarian?

CORTEZ: Idiot.

HAPPY: Wrong again You eat meat, don't you, Miss Cortez? We'll feed you meat. *(Pause)* Various groups have petitioned on your behalf. You're a celebrity. I'm in awe of celebrities. Does that make you feel happy? *(Pause)* You've very alluring eyes, Miss Cortez. Like harden diamonds in moonlight. They are the window into your soul. A privilege to see. Dear God, am I blushing? *(Pause)* I was told you know your rights, and that the McCarran-Walter Act was explained. Good. We can forego the long preamble. My government created McCarran-Walter to skim garbage off the surface of our shores. Senator McCarthy would be pleased to see the law thriving. It is a good law. According to my files, you don't belong here. You did wrong, Miss Cortez. You should have remained on the plane.

CORTEZ: My papers are in order.

HAPPY: The visa was issued in error. We wrote you, Miss Cortez. As an officer of Immigration and Naturalization, I wish to apologize for this incontrovertible error.

CORTEZ: Apologize?

HAPPY: The visa was rescinded. Tough luck.

CORTEZ: What are you afraid of? What has happened to America?

HAPPY: America has gotten stronger. More confident. *(Pause)* Are you a reporter for El Tiempo in Bogota? *(Pause)* It would help your case enormously, if you answer the questions. Are you a...

CORTEZ: Yes.

HAPPY: How many years?

CORTEZ: Eleven.

HAPPY: You don't look that old.

CORTEZ: I'm thirty seven.

HAPPY: Any children?

CORTEZ: No.

HAPPY: Your time clock is ticking, Miss Cortez.

CORTEZ: Don't lecture me, Mister Logan.

HAPPY: Are you a friend of democracy?

CORTEZ: I would hope so.

HAPPY: Do you know the meaning of democracy?

CORTEZ: More thoroughly than you.

HAPPY: Miss Cortez, are you an astrologist? Do you read Jean Dixon? *(Pause)* Miss Cortez, are you engaged in subversive activities in your native land? *(Pause)* Miss Cortez, do you like detention?

CORTEZ: Freedom is better than prison.

HAPPY: Exactly. Work with me, Miss Cortez. As a vegetarian I believe in tempered living. The golden mean. Christian sobriety. Are you a member of a Colombian group known as M-19?

CORTEZ: No.

HAPPY: Are you a Cuban agent?

CORTEZ: I am Jesus' sister.

HAPPY: I thought so. It says in my report that you served as a liason between M-19 and the Cuban secret police.

CORTEZ: I resent your accusations, Mister Logan.

HAPPY: The M-19 assaulted the Palace of Justice. Several deaths and many injuries. Play ball with us, Miss Cortez. In a few days you're expected at Harvard.

CORTEZ: I want my Ambassador.

HAPPY: Tell me you plan to cooperate, Miss Cortez.

CORTEZ: You shall not muzzle me.

HAPPY: Cooperate. Say it. Please.

CORTEZ: *(Pause)* I want to cooperate.

HAPPY: I believe you, Miss Cortez. My report says you're a renown columnist. Shrewd. Skillful. Tell me the truth. I know your wrongdoing. Your sins. My instructions are to crack you. I'm very good at this. I've many questions to ask you. Today. Tomorrow. The next day. Until the day I pour wine. I've other detainees waiting. You are number one. Prize catch in the net. Talk to me, Miss Cortez...

CORTEZ: What do you care to know?

HAPPY: Are you a virgin?

CORTEZ: Are you an imbecile?

HAPPY: Flatter my intelligence, Miss Cortez. I had a year of college. Are you a member of M-19?

CORTEZ: I want my lawyer.

HAPPY: We're holding your lawyer in other cell. I hate his cologne. You'll see him. I'd like to know about your personal life. Your personal contacts.

CORTEZ: I'm certain you have them in your reports.

HAPPY: I want names. Don't bother listing the academics. Men with guns. Names we fear. *(Starts tape recorder)* Go ahead, Miss Cortez.

CORTEZ: Go to hell.

HAPPY: It's my job, lovey.

CORTEZ: Are you so afraid of me, Mister Logan.

HAPPY: Do I seem afraid?

CORTEZ: Like a weasel, yes.

HAPPY: I'm not an animal, Miss Cortez.

CORTEZ: Scatch your private parts at home.

HAPPY: Give me ten names. That's all. And that will make me happy.

CORTEZ: You'll get no names.

HAPPY: Miss Cortez, now is the time to speak your mind.

CORTEZ: I don't like your administration's policies in Latin America. Your tacit support of Chile. The way your banks treat us. The deals made with El Salvador. The trade war with Cuba. Your games with Ortega and the Contras.

HAPPY: Have you killed people, Miss Cortez? Have you taught others to kill? Have you spent any time in Cuba? Did you have an affair with Gabriel Marquez at the Hilton in Buenos Aires? What is your sordid relationship with former President Belesario Bentancur? May we see an advance text of your Harvard address?

CORTEZ: Fuck off, Mister Logan.

HAPPY: I provoked a reaction. Forgive me. The tape was on. *(Turns off recorder)* May we please see an advance text, Miss Cortez?

CORTEZ: You've confiscated all my papers.

HAPPY: We could not find the Harvard address.

CORTEZ: For a free nation, your actions...

HAPPY: Are you a communist, Miss Cortez?

CORTEZ: No, Mister Logan.

HAPPY: A Marxist? A spider woman from Cuba? Is it true that you've served on the ruling committee of M-19?

CORTEZ: No.

HAPPY: Since we're getting nowhere, why not just give me some names, and we can stop this charade.

CORTEZ: For you?

HAPPY: Yes. For me. Because I sense that you secretly like me.

CORTEZ: Like you?

HAPPY: You know what I mean. *(Pause)* Some names. *(Pause)* Miss Cortez?

CORTEZ: Alright. *(Happy turns on tape)* Rockefeller... Forbes...Trump...Hunt...Getty...

HAPPY: *(Turns off tape)* Splendid. *(Pause)* Do you want a spanking? *(Pause)*

CORTEZ: I don't think I can satisfy you with this interrogation.

HAPPY: I should have been assigned to Cordoba. All I want is cooperation. *(Pause)* I was a postal employee for six years before getting transferred. My brother-in-law moved me into Immigration. Said the money was worth it. He didn't mention the aggrevation. Don't add to my aggravation. Miss Cortez, keep me happy. I know you can.

CORTEZ: I'm here to aggravate you.

HAPPY: Why did you choose to become a journalist?

CORTEZ: My father was a journalist.

HAPPY: Do you know Leonard Bernstein?

CORTEZ: No.

HAPPY: Ted Kennedy? Jane Fonda? Our agents discovered that you also had an appointment to visit East Hampton, Long Island. Can you corroborate that for me? It's off season in the Hamptons, Miss Cortez. What business do you have out there?

CORTEZ: A friend of my husband's has a country house.

HAPPY: A rich friend, no doubt?

CORTEZ: Richer than myself, yes.

HAPPY: You want publicity, to become a cause celibr<138>?

CORTEZ: No, Mister Logan.

HAPPY: You want to beat me, outsmart me. I can read your thoughts, Miss Cortez. I'm a formidable individual. I have your pulse. I feel the inexorable heat radiating from inside you. The Spanish paranoia in your voice. Give me credit for understanding you. For hunting you inside a small room. (*Silence. Smiling warmly*) Again, I only want names from you. What a simple deal it would be, if you only agreed to play the game. The game is simple, Miss Cortez. Come play the game.

Scene Two

(*Day one. Adjacent room*—AGUNEIR's *cell*)

AGUNEIR: Give me a cigarette.

FULLER: Here.

AGUNEIR: Match.

FULLER: On the table.

AGUNEIR: How long will this go on?

FULLER: I don't know.

AGUNEIR: You know. Cut the nonsense.

FULLER: J D L?

AGUNEIR: I'm not responsible for them.

FULLER: They were once your group.

AGUNEIR: Not now.

FULLER: There was a bombing last night. Cooperate, Aguneir.

AGUNEIR: I am an American.

FULLER: You hold two passports.

AGUNEIR: I was born in New York.

FULLER: You're an Israeli officer in the Knesset.

AGUNEIR: Until there's a change in the law, I am an American.

FULLER: Tell me, my friend, why you became violent at the airport? You punched out one of our officers. You were warned not to come.

AGUNEIR: Where is my insulin?

FULLER: Coming shortly.

AGUNEIR: I take it now, Fuller.

FULLER: Within the hour. What makes you an American? Your self-righteousness?

AGUNEIR: The Bible, you little asshole.

FULLER: Do you know the Bible so well?

AGUNEIR: I was an ordained Rabbi.

FULLER: Hard to believe.

AGUNEIR: Give me another cigarette.

FULLER: Take the pack.

AGUNEIR: You look at me with mockery.

FULLER: It's unintentional.

AGUNEIR: I'm not a madman.

FULLER: Prove it.

AGUNEIR: I'll walk on water.

FULLER: Tell me about the bombings.

AGUNEIR: There are bombings in Paris. Am I responsible?

FULLER: The Atlantic Avenue restaurant.

AGUNEIR: A diner's flatuence, I'm sure. I was in Israel during this period.

FULLER: What about the Defense League?

AGUNEIR: No contact with them in five years.

FULLER: You're full of shit.

AGUNEIR: All my energy is in Israel. You know that. Why are you keeping me here? Where is my insulin? When do I see my attorney Loveberg? I have friends in this city. Powerful friends. Soon I'll get on the phone.

FULLER: You call yourself the King of Israel.

AGUNEIR: No. Begin did.

FULLER: You're a lowlife.

AGUNEIR: I'm a glorious Sephardic saint. Get on your filthy knees. Where is your superior? Enough with this merry-go-round. I'm an important statesman. Get out of my way. Understand? Nod your head if you do. Give me your superior.

FULLER: You must deal with me. *(Pause)* Tell me about the munitions depot. Who was in charge?

AGUNEIR: An angel on earth. A pornographer from Beirut. Enough questions. I have no patience for this. Give me dinner. And then a clean taxi. I must go. And my insulin. I will call the Congressman from Long Island. I will punish you, God help you if you dally. I'm not a man of peace, I am a dark angel.

FULLER: What makes you a dark angel?

AGUNEIR: The world's a very sick place. *(Pause)* Who else have you locked here? *(Pause)* You should lock up Farrahkan. He hides a missile under his bow tie. Hitler's stepchild. Take racism where you find it.

FULLER: There's a rash of bombings with your visit.

AGUNEIR: There are bombings because people lack entertainment. They have no spiritual direction. Money can extend so far. Stick out your tongue, Fuller. Let's see how far you extend. *(He sticks out his tongue with obscene noise.)* I'm a religious leader lest you forget. And a hardcore politician. I can make the rudest

secular noises you ever heard. I am the new noise
in Israel. Why? Because I say what people hide in
their hearts. Because I herald from Brooklyn's Crown
Heights. Keep me locked up, you help my publicity.
Tell me what will you accomplish? I have a moral
agenda. You have an obscene shopping list.

FULLER: Give me a hint about the cash funds from
Jersey. The loan guarantees are in your name.

AGUNEIR: My name is artificial. Any guarantees are
artificial. I am self-invented. Pygmalion by Pygmalion.
My family name was Shulman. People use my name
for fund raising. My name attracts money. As it should.
I know you want to lay a trap for me. Go ahead. You're
dealing with a stubborn old man. I'll wait you out. I
am spirit, you see. You are clay. (Pause) I want to see a
newspaper, Fuller. Quick. Here's some change, go and
buy a paper. What is the press saying about this? Do
they know? Are they on your side, or mine?

FULLER: No newspapers.

AGUNEIR: Thief!

FULLER: Am I?

AGUNEIR: Where is my wristwatch?

FULLER: Did you have a wristwatch?

AGUNEIR: Yes. On the table.

FULLER: I don't have it.

AGUNEIR: It was given to me by my grandfather.
Empty your Goddamn pockets.

FULLER: Enough.

AGUNEIR: There's a putrid smell in this room.

FULLER: I think it's time to straighten you out. You're
not in Israel. While you're here, you must give
answers. I'm running out of patience. And that's a

bad thing. You can only start trouble here. I'm not a negotiator. I don't bargain. There have been a dozen bombings in the last month. J D L related. And now you're here. The timing stinks. Bombs going off like roman candles in the night. Somthing's scaring this city, and we're going to eradicate it. *(Pause)* I don't like you Aguneir. I don't like your blatant supremacy airs. You look very ugly to me. It's the pathology of your rabid face which I hate.

AGUNEIR: You've no reason to hate me.

FULLER: You're a racist and demigogue.

AGUNEIR: I'm a member of clergy. I herd my flock.

FULLER: Such garbage with no love in your heart.

AGUNEIR: Not true. I love all people. Rich and poor. White and Black. I love you.

FULLER: Do you?

AGUNEIR: Ethiopians are my brethren. You may be a Jew, Fuller. Come, I'll circumcise you.

FULLER: *(Leaving bag on table. Rising)* You're an actor from Hell. When I come back, I want some answers about these punks in your old neighborhood. It can be much easier to comply. Talk quickly, and with respect. *(Exiting)* Your insulin is in the bag.

Scene Three

(Next Day. CORTEZ's room)

HAPPY: You look like my wife's sister, Miss Cortez. A little arrogant and heavy on the eye shadow. It's the way you drum your fingers on the table. And your garish nail polish. My wife's sister has a piercing cold stare. Right to my heart. She eats men and spits them out like cherry pits. Not my idea of a dream girl.

CORTEZ: What is your idea of a dream girl, Mister Logan?

HAPPY: I like my slippers brought to the foot of the bed.

CORTEZ: Get a German Shepard.

HAPPY: My dream girl would be someone who brings me inner peace. Like the girls from the orient. Someone to draw the warm bath. And keep evil spirits from the front door. An angel who doesn't spend a ton of money. But you see, Miss Cortez, I'm already married. Surely you've noticed my wedding ring? *(Pause)* A woman should flatter the opposite sex. As you are, I'm sure, quite capable of doing. Because you are the smarter sex. I've always felt that. You know the weaknesses in men. You know the subtleties of psychology. Isn't that so? How can I compete with you in this arena? *(Pause)* Tell me, Miss Cortez, why would Harvard honor you if you're known in astute circles as Castro's ass-licking whore?

CORTEZ: And you bend over for Reagan.

HAPPY: He's my President.

CORTEZ: He's living a movie. I think that's dangerous.

HAPPY: I think your radicalism is dangerous.

CORTEZ: My radicalism is in print. I don't shoot people.

HAPPY: What do you do in bed?

CORTEZ: What do you do in the bathroom, Mister Logan?

HAPPY: I read the newspaper. *(Pause)* Did you ever perform felatio in public on an army rifle? Smile, Miss Cortez. Behind that mirror, there's a camera on you. Because when you're gone, I'll have something of you still with me. I'm a collector. And you will have joined my collection. *(Pause)* Your profile in black and white.

Your fingers tapping the wood. No one in the room but you. You put on a different face alone. A face of insecurity.

CORTEZ: I must be human, Mister Logan.

HAPPY: Indeed you are. *(Pause)* Miss Cortez, you look drowsy today. Is it that time of month? Would you like Midol? *(Pause)* We're going to make a deal with you. We want you to attend Harvard's convocation. Escorted, first class, cocktails and dinner. All this provided by Immigration.

CORTEZ: What's the deal?

HAPPY: I get to be your handsome escort.

CORTEZ: You?

HAPPY: Because I volunteered. And we're going to dress you in new clothes, because we've ripped your dresses.

CORTEZ: Why are you changing tactics?

HAPPY: Does it seem that way?

CORTEZ: It would be scandalous to your administration if I fail to show.

HAPPY: No, Miss Cortez.

CORTEZ: You inept boy scout.

HAPPY: I had a very unhappy childhood. Does it show?

CORTEZ: I want to see a newspaper.

HAPPY: When we go to the airport.

CORTEZ: Let my ambassador escort me.

HAPPY: Your Ambassador?

CORTEZ: He's a political conservative. What could be safer?

HAPPY: I think you're a dangerous communist, Miss Cortez. Alarms go off in my head. The world may applaud your writing, but it is a free world which I seek to maintain. I must escort you to protect your freedom of speech. Call it magnamity. A special leniency. Thank me when my job is done.

CORTEZ: You're a blithering idiot.

HAPPY: And what are you, Miss Cortez?

CORTEZ: A Social Democrat.

HAPPY: If I slap your lovely powdered face, a red soldier would feel pain. Who is the real underdog, Miss Cortez? Who is the pretender?

CORTEZ: I'll make certain this incident is made known.

HAPPY: Take out an ad in *The New York Times*.

CORTEZ: Harvard will suffice.

HAPPY: You'll accept the prize from a wheelchair. Word is out that you fell in the shower. Because of painkillers, you cannot speak.

CORTEZ: Even if you gag me, this will explode in your face.

HAPPY: And you're such a fine writer to take on the subject. You're a pert gal, Miss Cortez. I really wish you were on our side. Really, with a little encouragement, I would nuzzle you. Entreat your husband. Have children. Isn't that what nature wants of you? Obedience and fertility. Put down your pen and start breast feeding. Politics is too costly. *(Pause)* I would like to take you on a walking tour of the city. Show you the Staten Island ferry and the harbor. But you look at me with such disdain. *(Pause)* We're moving you to a new room for the rest of the weekend. You'll have a window with a view of the courtyard. You'll see a delightful French marble.

CORTEZ: I'm not going to Harvard with you, Mister Logan.

HAPPY: Dinner plans tonight will be a gala affair. Some dignitaries from Washington want to meet you. To convince you to see the good things in the United States. Senator Helms and friends. They want a door to your special world, Miss Cortez. Give them entrance. They want good things for Colombia. See them. It would be a feather in my cap.

CORTEZ: Perhaps there's another arrangement more dignified, Mister Logan? Dignity is why I write, why I breathe. Can you understand the word?

HAPPY: Dignity...no one can take from you.

CORTEZ: You have no dignity, Mister Logan. What did you do to Cordoba?

HAPPY: A deal very similar to yours.

CORTEZ: Did she approve?

HAPPY: Go ask her. You may be eating dinner together alfresco.

CORTEZ: With Cordoba?

HAPPY: Yes, under candlelight on an elegant white table cloth, with missing body parts of guerrilla fighters.

CORTEZ: Your jokes are obscene.

HAPPY: Better obscene than dated.

CORTEZ: Better obscene than dead.

HAPPY: Who's dead, Miss Cortez?

CORTEZ: A friend in Bogota. An assassination. Seven bullets to the head. A brother to my brother.

HAPPY: I'm very sorry. Death never comes justly.

CORTEZ: In my hometown, we have a tradition of walking to the ocean for the New Year. Everyone takes this walk. We walk at night, for the certain belief that our sins will wash into the sea. We all believe

this. It seems to make us feel better inside. I miss this
tradition, Mister Logan. It is something which I lost
when I became a journalist. My loss. *(Pause)* In my
hometown we have a saying: To know your deed,
know your partner. It always made little sense to
me. Always. My mind gets cranky, and bitter. I don't
want to become another burnt cynic. I'm very angry
inside. Angry at Yankee games with our economy and
autonomy. My dearest friends are getting killed.

HAPPY: Get off your soap box.

CORTEZ: Get off my back. I'm no threat to you, Mister
Logan.

HAPPY: You're like Joan of Arc with castanets.

CORTEZ: Send me back to Colombia. I owe you no
favor. This investigation is over.

HAPPY: Solitude is yours for the asking. Listen to
your heels in the corner of the night, grind your teeth
through insomnia. Suffer for your vanity.

CORTEZ: Don't eye me, Mister Logan.

HAPPY: Your beauty charms me. You've a swan's neck.

*(*HAPPY *touches* CORTEZ's *neck. She slaps him)*

HAPPY: Under different circumstances, I would wine
you and dine you. Court you like Sir Walter Raleigh.
I am a romantic. Ballroom dancing and moonlight
serenades. Tempting the low hem of your skirt, fluffing
your pleats, spreading your natural wings. Sing poetry
in your Latin ear. Tonight our cook is serving Paella on
yellow rice.

CORTEZ: Look away, Mister Logan. I am a married
woman. It means something to me. I expect to be in
Colombia soon. This turgid affair has gone on too long.
Insults bear stupidity. You must act quickly or lose

your prey. I've no more patience for your cheapness.
Act quickly with me. Or else. *Comprende?*

Scene Four

(Next Day. AGUNEIR's *room)*

FULLER: Game Three of the World Series is on tonight.
I'm not going to babysit for you, my man. We need
to work real quick. *(Pause)* A Congressman came
today. We told him you had returned to Jerusalem.
He believed us. You think we act like dime store
detectives, and suddenly we fulfill your expectations.

AGUNEIR: When I'm through with you, Fuller, you'll be
a waiter in the Catskills.

FULLER: I'll kick your ass, pal. It gives me satisfaction to
detain a bigot with such small gonads.

AGUNEIR: I am no bigot.

FULLER: But you want to expel the Palestinians.

AGUNEIR: They have cousin states. Israel is for Jews.

FULLER: What sort of Jew are you?

AGUNEIR: I am a Rabbi. Yes, a learned man. I could
teach you Talmud, or self-defense. Soul and armor. I
could beat your brains out. Listen to me, Fuller, I've
family waiting. Release me. I'll sing your name to
Heaven and I'll grease your palm.

FULLER: I understand you have a girlfriend in the city.

AGUNEIR: And if I do?

FULLER: Tell me what she's like.

AGUNEIR: She's uniquely feminine.

FULLER: Is she political?

AGUNEIR: I just told you, bozo. She's very feminine.

FULLER: I understand she likes rough games.

AGUNEIR: Fuck yourself.

FULLER: Do you like rough games, Rabbi? Is it in the Talmud?

AGUNEIR: Don't play with me, yo yo.

FULLER: We're going to move you to another place, Aguneir.

AGUNEIR: You need to hide me. You're losing.

FULLER: I never lose.

AGUNEIR: The Congressman from Long Island will find me. And then you'll be thrown on your black ass.

FULLER: Why did you come to New York?

AGUNEIR: To see my girl and get laid.

FULLER: She thinks you should fly back to Israel. You're begging for trouble. It's not a good year for certain Jews.

AGUNEIR: I'm not a certain Jew.

FULLER: I think your girlfriend makes a whole lot of sense.

AGUNEIR: I don't like advice from colored people.

FULLER: Aguneir, we're going to hold you until hell freezes over. Until your attitude improves. And I will gloat.

AGUNEIR: Do you have the heart to gloat?

FULLER: Watch me.

AGUNEIR: I think you're chicken shit. You remind me of a group of people in Israel. You remind me of the cab drivers in their stained tank tops. You remind me of the discount merchants. You remind me of the lackeys in the civilian army. Your ludicrous bravado. You're a jackass of dubious talents. Little gut. No class. A low level traffic cop. But you have that affinity for cheap prizes and vulgarity. I am not a cheap prize. Get that through your knappy black head. I am not garbage. In this room, you share space with a very holy man. Genuflect, like a good cocksucker, and get out of my life.

FULLER: *(Firmly, but restrained)* Well, time's up. Get your things, Aguneir. Put them inside that paper bag. Quickly. We're moving your ass now. You'll miss this room. Believe me, you will.

Scene Five

(Thursday. Staff lounge)

FULLER: Watching the World Series? Big upset.

HAPPY: Got money on the game?

FULLER: Couple of bucks. Why so down?

HAPPY: I'm alright. Wearing new shoes. Like the fashion? Italian look.

FULLER: Italian?

HAPPY: Yeah, Italian. Pinches like shit, but looks great. Thought my wife would like me in them. I'm sick of looking like a slob. You're as good as you look. As good as you feel. I look at your shoes, Fuller, and you know what I see?

FULLER: What?

HAPPY: No ambition.

FULLER: From my shoes?

HAPPY: No shit.

FULLER: I like my shoes.

HAPPY: And you know what? Your vests are out of style. You look like a train conductor, Fuller. Come

on. I'll take you shopping. I know a good chink tailor
on Essex Street. I hate expensive clothes. If you got
the right crease in your trouser...the right fold over
the shoe...the right roll of the lapel...I'm talking about
sophistication in a worsted blend. And shirts with
French cuffs. Clothes you wouldn't dare perspire in.
(Pause) Hey, Fuller, do you think I shop at Barney's?
Do you think I shoplift?

FULLER: Coffee?

HAPPY: Yeah.

FULLER: You look preoccupied.

HAPPY: Me?

FULLER: You.

HAPPY: Preoccupied?

FULLER: Yeah.

HAPPY: It's been three days.

FULLER: Any progress?

HAPPY: Only with the spic.

FULLER: Cordoba?

HAPPY: The other broad, Cortez, La Bruja with the
serpent's tongue.

FULLER: How hard you drilling?

HAPPY: Shit, I've been too gentle. I might spike her
food. And you?

FULLER: No rough stuff. All routine.

HAPPY: Though I wouldn't kick her out of bed, you
know what I mean? Saucy dish. Would love to dive
into her muff. You know the fantasy. A little souvenir.
(Produced pink panties to his nose) From her hamper. A
fragrance for Oscar De Laurenta.

FULLER: Right.

HAPPY: When are you up for vacation?

FULLER: December, for the holidays.

HAPPY: Lucky you.

FULLER: I received a call from a few Congressmen. Another sub-committee survey.

HAPPY: Are they coming?

FULLER: Yes.

HAPPY: Fuck 'em all. Every asshole wants to be a reformer. Just what we need.

FULLER: Show and tell time.

HAPPY: Put on a clean necktie, Fuller. Bark on cue. They want shiny smiles.

FULLER: I won't be able to crack Aguneir in time.

HAPPY: The Jew's a real prick.

FULLER: You bet.

HAPPY: Son of a bitch. We ought to play *Hava Nagilah* on a tape loop. Drive the kike nuts. Or feed him pork.

FULLER: If this goes another day or two, I'm sending him back.

HAPPY: Then your average slips. We're on the big board, Fuller.

FULLER: I know, Happy.

HAPPY: My average's gone up five months straight. Fuller, I'm on a fucking roll. Going to get some big mother perks this Christmas.

FULLER: Don't flaunt it, okay?

HAPPY: I'm enjoying myself. Makes all the difference. We've a noble cause, to protect our Constitution. The subversive element will outspend us, outsmart us, always outrage us. Got to draw the line. God blessed our country. As caretakers to her gate, we must keep a

vigilant eye and an iron hand. And you must enjoy the
challenge...be he terrorist, commie or Jew.

FULLER: Where does it say we must bust heads?

HAPPY: I don't make the rules, and you're no rookie,
babe.

FULLER: When I took this job, Hooper broke me in. Said
to play fair. We have authority to weed out the bad
apples. No one mentioned cracking to the breaking
point. He mentioned civil liberties.

HAPPY: For citizens. For harmless visitors. For us,
cracking is everything. Otherwise we're custom
officials. You need smarts. Cracking is a surgical skill.
A pogrom against the mind of our enemies. Asserts our
rights to govern in an hostile world. You know they do
this to our people.

FULLER: Yeah.

HAPPY: Daniloff in Moscow. Hausenfaus in Nicaragua.
Terbin in Korea. They bomb our Embassies, freeze
our Swiss bank accounts, make fools of our Marines.
Cracking immunes us from political disease.

FULLER: *(Sarcastic)* Run for office, Happy.

HAPPY: I'm not a panzy, Fuller. You have compassion
for the wrong assholes.

FULLER: How do you know?

HAPPY: When we go to parties together, I see how you
act. You go soft and tender. I read people well. Some
people have this gift. I'm shrewder than you.

FULLER: I have a conscience, Happy.

HAPPY: So do I. Don't get lofty, asshole. Sometimes you
have to choose between patriotism and conscience. I
don't mean to insult you. Let's toughen up.

FULLER: Do me a favor. Take my man. Celebrity swap.

HAPPY: The Jew?

FULLER: I'll cover Cortez.

HAPPY: Want me to be your point man?

FULLER: Aguneir won't break. Not with me. Sweet talk an Israeli? Don't know what button to push. Cortez is more my style. I'll owe you one, Happy.

HAPPY: Tickets to the Garden?

FULLER: Alright.

HAPPY: These twits are all the same to me. We chop them down and ship them out. It's a deal.

(FULLER *and* HAPPY *nod to each other.* HAPPY *lights cigarette, then discards it.*)

HAPPY: My wife ran away last night, Fuller. She's seeing somebody while I work late. I give her my checks. I never ask for anything in return. I went shopping for her. What a cunt. Has my mind all bent out. Tells me I'm in metabolic decline. Mister Rust. What's a guy to do, Fuller? I'm young and well hung. With a little help, I can get it up. If this continues, I plan to kill the little missus. I'll staple her head to our wedding album. You know the feeling, man? When the audacity cuts through your heart with the coldest blade. The asinine smile of deceit in her eyes. I give her one last chance. I can be liberal, Fuller. I still love her madly. *(Pause)* Your wife is faithful.

FULLER: Yeah.

HAPPY: How come?

FULLER: I go home early and take care of business. Attentiveness. Magic word. *(Pause)* Give it time, Happy. What the hell happened to your ears?

HAPPY: *(Pointing to tape marks along his earlobes)* These? Acupuncture.

FULLER: For what?

HAPPY: Therapy.

FULLER: Therapy?

HAPPY: For impotence. *(Laughs)* For smoking. Trying to kick it altogether. Almost burned myself in bed last week.

FULLER: Is it working?

HAPPY: *(Demonstrating)* You got to rub them every once in a while. Whenever the urge comes. Stimulates the nerves. I feel a change. Makes me civil. I don't smoke much around here. I just rub my Goddamn ears.

FULLER: And it makes you happy?

HAPPY: Who the fuck knows.

FULLER: Take the Israeli, Happy. He's a madman. You're the pro. Give me the keys to your girlfriend's room. I'll see Miss Cortez.

(HAPPY tosses keys to FULLER.)

Scene Six

(Later that day. AGUNEIR's room)

AGUNEIR: Who the hell are you?

HAPPY: Agent Logan, United States Immigration.

AGUNEIR: Where's the other idiot?

HAPPY: Re-assignment.

AGUNEIR: What are you, the designated hitter?

HAPPY: I'm here to make you more comfortable.

AGUNEIR: I want color television and a Jacuzzi. Quick, yo-yo.

HAPPY: Anything else?

AGUNEIR: I want my insulin.

HAPPY: No more insulin. Drug store just closed.

AGUNEIR: Listen, I'm not a young man like yourself. I can't tolerate these clubhouse games. The colored man didn't like me. You won't either.

HAPPY: You had asked for his supervisor.

AGUNEIR: I'm to have insulin every morning. Clean food. And I want my personal things back. I pray each morning with my prayer book and shawl.

HAPPY: A vegetarian lives longer, has finer bowel movements, and maintains a superior memory. Are you a vegetarian? *(Pause)* Why do you pray? Tell me, I'm curious. When you carry such hatred, how do you expect God to hear your prayers?

AGUNEIR: Because my prayers have passion.

HAPPY: And so do mine. And I pray all the time. For peace in this world. I pray for all the world's children. Yours and mine. I'm a spiritual person, even as I work for the government. And I'm a happy spirit. We need more happy spirits. Why not be one? *(Pause)* Talk to me. I know nothing about you. What is Judaism? Or militancy? You're not a typical Jew. You've got a set of balls. *(Pause)* There was another bombing last night.

AGUNEIR: I know nothing about it.

HAPPY: A small Arab child is now in critical condition at the hospital.

AGUNEIR: I'm very sorry.

HAPPY: Are you?

AGUNEIR: I am.

HAPPY: I don't believe you.

AGUNEIR: Believe what you want.

HAPPY: Agent Fuller—the colored man—was exceptionally kind to you.

AGUNEIR: In this world, one can never be too kind.

HAPPY: How kind should I be?

AGUNEIR: Give me my insulin. *(Pause)* I know who you are. I know.

HAPPY: I'm going to crack your skull like a walnut, Rabbi.

AGUNEIR: *(Indifferent. Removes tobacco)* Cigarette?

HAPPY: I'm trying to quit.

AGUNEIR: Menthol. Won't kill you.

HAPPY: *(Snatches it from AGUNEIR's mouth)* Eat the cigarette.

AGUNEIR: *(Removes second cigarette)* Mister Logan, You're dealing with an elected member of the Israeli Knesset. A political dignitary. Surely, you've reached puberty? *(Happy snatches cigarette)* I sense you don't respect me.

HAPPY: I hate Jews like you.

AGUNEIR: What are we going to do about that?

HAPPY: I want the fucking bombings to stop.

AGUNEIR: Didn't the colored man tell you I don't squeal? I hold up very well. You won't. I know you. Is it money that you want? How much, Mister Logan? I'll lubricate you.

HAPPY: How much?

AGUNEIR: Rich man I'm not. But name an amount. This I did not offer the other agent. Tell me your price.

HAPPY: Fifty thousand.

AGUNEIR: Alright.

HAPPY: How would I get it?

AGUNEIR: From my bank in Manhattan.

HAPPY: I can't go to a bank.

AGUNEIR: I'm not free to get it, Mister Logan.

HAPPY: Ask someone to go for you. And have them come here.

AGUNEIR: Perhaps.

HAPPY: Give me his name.

AGUNEIR: I can't. It's too dangerous.

HAPPY: Deal's off.

AGUNEIR: You talk to me like I work in the garment district. We must be discreet, Mister Logan, lest we risk a misunderstanding.

HAPPY: What is his name?

AGUNEIR: His name is Ed.

HAPPY: Ed what?

AGUNEIR: The comic. Ed Koch. I can vouch for him.

HAPPY: *(Grabs* AGUNEIR's *lapels)* Don't jerk me around, Aguneir!

AGUNEIR: Let go of me.

HAPPY: *(Slaps* AGUNEIR*)* Time's running out.

AGUNEIR: You're worse than the colored man. He had manners.

HAPPY: *(Menacing)* I have manners. You're going to see my manners.

AGUNEIR: *(Calmly)* Drop dead, Mister Logan.

HAPPY: Deep down, every Jew's a villian. Born an American. Military service. University degrees. You leave your native country. Dubious Zionistic goals. A racist. Your file shows a history of mental instability. Do you talk to yourself when left alone?

AGUNEIR: I'm talking to myself right now.

HAPPY: You know me.

AGUNEIR: Yes.

HAPPY: Then be afraid of me. I've a very short fuse.

AGUNEIR: Do you?

HAPPY: You shoot Arabs.

AGUNEIR: Nonsense.

HAPPY: *(Pulling* AGUNEIR's *hair back)* Answer me.

AGUNEIR: No.

HAPPY: You have no moral conscience. *(Pushing* AGUNEIR's *head to one side)*

AGUNEIR: *(Recovering)* Mister Logan, what is the point of these brilliant questions? *(Pause)* You bore me. The interrogation's over.

HAPPY: If there is one more bombing, I'm going to scramble your brains with a wooden spoon.

AGUNEIR: How can I stop the bombings?

HAPPY: Pray. Nod your ugly Yiddish head and pray. I'm not the colored man. You damn well better pray.

Scene Seven

(Fourth day. CORTEZ's *room)*

CORTEZ: I'm quite ill.

FULLER: I know.

CORTEZ: I've diarrhea. Fever. Spasms.

FULLER: We gave it to you. In the food. Salmonella. *(Pause)* If you'd like, we can get you a medic.

CORTEZ: Yes.

FULLER: All our medics are good.

CORTEZ: I'm sure.

FULLER: This is as far as I'll push you. I've read your list of names. They read more or less complete.

CORTEZ: Logan appeared satisfied.

FULLER: Yes. We play good cop, bad cop routines.

CORTEZ: Which cop are you?

FULLER: The good cop.

CORTEZ: Is it that you want names, or the sheer satisfaction of seeing my corporal body contorted? You've made me sick and weak. Resorting to food poison. If you have any decency...use physical force. Is it because I am a woman?

FULLER: Everything's a factor.

CORTEZ: Your partner's not very bright. You seem more refined.

FULLER: Do I?

CORTEZ: You're a cautious man, Mister Fuller. I see it in your countinance. I see your crude strategies on your face. Perhaps it's because I have severe cramps and delirium. In jail, many things are possible. One either finds renewed strength or weakness. Did I seem easy to you?

FULLER: No.

CORTEZ: Did I do so much to merit this descent? Was it a sneer? A mischosen word in some obscure newspaper? Well, well, well, my diarrhea speaks to me most eloquently. Mister Fuller, if you were me... and I you...would depression set in? Despondency? Would you cave in? Write tawdry poems of despair on the prison walls? Imagine a B-movie based on your squalor.

FULLER: Consider yourself lucky.

CORTEZ: You let them exploit you.

FULLER: I'm doing my job.

CORTEZ: And you fed shit to Angelica?

FULLER: I'm not allowed to say.

CORTEZ: Your sympathies are for the wrong people. Whom do you have locked up next door?

FULLER: An Israeli.

CORTEZ: I can hear him at night, screaming madly. Crying like a child. What's in his bowels? Are you beating the daylights out of him?

FULLER: No one's beating him.

CORTEZ: I think you're beating him around the clock. Is it like Argentina in the Seventies? Are you beating him with American magazines?

FULLER: Israelis are remarkable tough creatures.

CORTEZ: What prevented my own beatings, Mister Fuller?

FULLER: I stepped in.

CORTEZ: Should I believe you?

FULLER: You gave us significant information.

CORTEZ: I gave you names of little consequence. Names you never needed. I'm very ill, Mister Fuller. I hate to mess. Where is this indispensible medic?

FULLER: Somewhere in the building.

CORTEZ: The names I gave you...I regret. You will get no more names. How wretched I feel. For being civil with you. My fever rises. Did you feed me cat's piss? Your mother's cooking? I don't understand your country. Last year I arrived in New York without incident. I don't understand the paranoia. What a mystery it is. I have a sister here, in Boston. Well, you know this. She knows this country. Is not shocked by it. It may be cultural. It may be utter capriciousness. Mister Fuller, you people have fortified my passions. My mind has formed certain blisters. In time they will burst. Mister Fuller, I need the bathroom now. Unlock the door. A spasm of stomach pain. *(Pause)* You have to open the door for me.

(FULLER *rises.*)

CORTEZ: Such chivalry. You are a gentleman.

Scene Eight

(Later that day. Lounge)

FULLER: What the hell are you doing?

HAPPY: *(Rolling marijuana)* Coffee break. Hell of a day, Fuller. The claustrophobia gets out of hand. Need a window. A little weed, medicinal. Like tea to the English. Subliminal. Transcendental. The home remedies we seek. *(Lights up)* We're not on earth to suffer. There's no point to pain. That's why I come home late each night. Long strolls at the mall. A toke. It's my beatific marriage. She stays in the bathroom for hours. The neurotic accusations. The price we pay for working late, for eating alone, for combing the house for clues, for masterbating while she sleeps. The long days without gratification. There must be an escape.

FULLER: Trout fishing.

HAPPY: What?

FULLER: Fishing is very calm. Quiet rivers. Natural sounds. The flight of birds.

HAPPY: Too fucking dull, Fuller. I need tumult. Bam, bam, bam. Aquaduct and the flats. O T B. Fucking action. Hot winners. Talking dirty to a ditsy blonde at the track. Wrapping her thighs around the broadest

smile on earth. Drinking life. Fishing? Hell, Fuller, I'm
a scuba diver. *(Extending cigarette to* FULLER*)* A toke,
Mister Straight?

FULLER: No.

HAPPY: Don't judge me, Fuller. I'm going through a
period of tension.

FULLER: I don't judge people, man.

HAPPY: How's my Spanish girlfriend?

FULLER: Recovering, though the diarrhea's still severe.

HAPPY: Medic came?

FULLER: An hour ago.

HAPPY: She'll drop a couple of pounds. She'll thank us.

FULLER: I think we pissed her off.

HAPPY: We broke her like a house puppy. She cowered
to us. Sends one on the grandest ego trip.

FULLER: Not me.

HAPPY: You get off on it, Fuller. I've seen it. *(Pause)*
Because you're just like me. We're the same shit.
(Pause) When I get stoned, Fuller, I feel all the
Goddamn wrinkles fall out. I feel freedom, love for
humanity. I think about the glorious Sixties. The
flowers and simple pink nudity. Big fucking tits
and gorgeous sun flowers with Van Gogh and Jimi
Hendrix. A return trip from Saigon. *(Pause)* Come,
take a hit. *(Pause)* I would hate to be locked in this
jail, Fuller. Makes me fucking blue. No clocks. No
vents. The fucking odors here. The hidden mikes
behind the corrugated ceiling tile. Polygraphs up the
ass. Telegrams from Washington pushing for speed.
Pushing us harder. Just pushing too far. The mind is a
complicated lock. So fucking hard to pick. Everyone's
picking someone's brains. *(Pause)* Cortez is such a Latin

cocktease. Her black pantyhose, Fuller. You know what I mean.

FULLER: You're falling in love with her, shithead.

HAPPY: Can you tell?

FULLER: I know you very well.

HAPPY: We spent a few years together.

FULLER: A few years.

HAPPY: We're a team, buddy. A terrific fucking team.

FULLER: Go easy on that stuff.

HAPPY: The Israeli is fucking us up. We finish him off now. He's not getting his insulin. I've made a switch.

FULLER: On whose authority?

HAPPY: My own.

FULLER: I don't know, Happy.

HAPPY: I've twenty four hours to deadline.

FULLER: Do you want to team up on him? You look wiped out.

HAPPY: No, I'm staying all night, Fuller.

FULLER: Why?

HAPPY: To surprise the ballbusting Jew. It's got to happen by tonight.

FULLER: Don't go overboard. You're putting in too many hours.

HAPPY: I've got fucking stamina.

FULLER: Stamina for what?

HAPPY: Stamina to mount the head of this militant Jew. Not because he's a mad zealot. Not because he plays us for little idiots. I do it for kicks. A sport. I am the watchdog for Liberty.

FULLER: Your eyes are so fucking bloodshot. You look like shit.

HAPPY: I'm going to crack him tonight. My honor. I won't sleep. Going to teach him the waltz and sweep the cell clean. *(Pause)* Submission. *(Pause)* And then I'll celebrate with Miss Latin American. Party time. Come on, Fuller, doesn't she turn you on?

FULLER: Go home.

HAPPY: No.

FULLER: Go home, Happy.

HAPPY: Fuller... *(Steady eye contact. In a moment)* I can't. There's someone with Joyce tonight.

FULLER: How do you know?

HAPPY: I head on the extension phone.

FULLER: I'm sorry.

HAPPY: I'd go home to break his goddamn neck, but the asshole's six foot two and an amateur boxer. I'm not looking for humiliation in my fucking living room. My home life is down the tubes. *(Pause)* Get the fuck out of here, Fuller.

Scene Nine

(Fifth day. AGUNEIR's *room.* AGUNEIR's *face is severely bruised)*

FULLER: Are you alright? I can call the medic. We have pain killers. *(Pause)* My partner was under pressure. One too many bombings. He means well. I'm very sorry for what happened. I guarantee you, it won't happen again.

AGUNEIR: Go to hell.

FULLER: He simply ran out of time. His methods are not my methods. I should have stayed with you last night. I could have guessed this.

(FULLER *offers cigarette to* AGUNEIR, *who accepts*)

FULLER: Agent Logan completed your release forms. Apparently, you played ball with him. I'm very glad. As soon as your face heals, we're going to fly you back to Jerusalem. Obviously, you can't remain in the States. *(Pause)* They tell me vitamin E is good for skin wounds. Would you like to try some? *(Produces vial of tablets)* Well, I'll leave them with you. Agent Logan has turned you over to me for the duration of your stay. Naturally, I will do everything I can to make you feel comfortable. Our job is done. Except for the formalities. *(Pause)* Is there anything I can do for you, Mister Aguneir? Mister Aguneir?

AGUNEIR: I want to leave now.

FULLER: But your face...

AGUNEIR: I'll wear sunglasses.

FULLER: We can't allow that.

AGUNEIR: Then get the hell out of my sight.

FULLER: I never meant you any harm.

AGUNEIR: What he did to me, you are an accomplice. In God's eyes. In my eyes.

FULLER: I meant you no harm.

AGUNEIR: Only the finest hospitality. Last night was my Sabbath. You violated my Sabbath. You've desecrated my own person. You spit on my soul. Get out of here. Logan stole my medicine. You rupture me with total contempt. What are you looking at? Get out of here! I gave you information. So get out of here. I was born in this country. I fought in Korea. And you shit on me. Get out, Fuller. I can't urinate.

FULLER: I'll send in the medic.

AGUNEIR: Send in a Rabbi. *(Pause)* You heard me. *(Pause)* You must relish my humiliation.

FULLER: No.

AGUNEIR: My bedsheets are soiled.

FULLER: I'll have them changed.

AGUNEIR: Am I to believe that you're the moderate among the American Nazis? You practice no restraints? Logan is your superior?

FULLER: Yes.

AGUNEIR: And he does what he wants?

FULLER: Within limits.

AGUNEIR: And you say nothing about it?

FULLER: What should I say?

AGUNEIR: Each man owns a conscience.

FULLER: Yes.

AGUNEIR: For a colored man, you're quite accommodating. You should be sensitive to human rights. Not compromising what you hold as common decency. But you get by. You survive, tail between your legs. Pathetic. Logan is a monster. Your half-wit superior. He makes hideous racial jokes about you. Yes. I find it very offensive.

FULLER: He bad mouths for a reason.

AGUNEIR: What's the reason?

FULLER: He flies off the handle, that's all.

AGUNEIR: I don't like nigger jokes, Mister Fuller. Believe what you want. I tell you, your colleague's a racist and a demon.

FULLER: And what are you?

AGUNEIR: I am now crippled.

FULLER: Nonsense.

AGUNEIR: Fuck you. *(Pause)* I am a separatist. There are nations which must house minorities. There are nations which dominate minorities. This is not the time to instruct you, Mister Fuller, about the Diaspora. But the Bible says I am right. So I am a separatist. By necessity. Every government in history has punished my people. My world stands apart from others. And I'm outspoken about it. Colored people have suffered too. So you know the deeper truths. Yes? A man like Logan knifes you in the back. I don't. Which do you prefer? *(Pause)* What sort of friendship have you with him? He cares for you like a Bircher. Like a lyncher. Like the hooded figure behind a gasoline cross. You are a colossal fool.

FULLER: I'll get the medic.

AGUNEIR: Ask him. Go see. Get burned. Burn him.

FULLER: You're delirious.

AGUNEIR: I speak the truth. You cannot be coy about a hatred. What happens when a black nationalist comes to New York? Do you drag him here? Do you take liberties? Beat him senseless? Do you draw straws for each turn?

FULLER: Conserve your strength.

AGUNEIR: You and your partner belong in the Middle Ages during the Holy Terror. God will foil you when a sudden fright jumps out of your skin.

FULLER: My job's important to me. I take it quite seriously. We provide a necessary service to national security. Rude as it might seem to you.

AGUNEIR: I think you're full of shit.

FULLER: You're entitled to think what you want.

AGUNEIR: I think persecuted people should carry guns under their jackets and shoot without hesitation all government officials. I think your magnificent xenophobia has exceeded all thresholds. I think you and your squinty eye partner will live forever in this pig dungeon. I think you know the depth of my recalcitrant feelings.

FULLER: Yes, I think I do. *(Pause)* You're turning color.

AGUNEIR: No matter how badly you paint me, and curse me, I have sovereignty over my life and well being. Bandages and all. There is a sick man in this cot. I will nail your partner, Mister Fuller. I swear to you, as God is my witness, I will. I will make him swallow his wicked little tongue. He will choke. Now fetch your Goddamn medic before I explode inside.

Scene Ten

(Day five. CORTEZ's room)

HAPPY: You're leaving us, Miss Cortez. I'm so glad to give you the news. A little smile for the gentleman? *(Pause)* You've lost weight, I see. Aged. What a woman loses in beauty, she gains in character. How good to release you in time for the holiday weekend. I personally thank you for assisting our investigation. Some of your information was invaluable to our work. In the short time we became acquainted, I grew to understand your politics, your diction, your perfume, and your unique personal struggles. *(Pause)* I was moved, Miss Cortez. How rare that is. And how strange to be telling you this. To trust you at this stage. To feel tenderness. *(Pause)* Any questions?

CORTEZ: Where do I go?

HAPPY: Back to Colombia, of course.

CORTEZ: I've seen the morning newspapers.

HAPPY: Yes?

CORTEZ: Your Under-Secretary of State has branded me in the blackest of colors. You know I risk reprisals in my city from this adverse publicity.

HAPPY: Oh, come now, Miss Cortez...

CORTEZ: There are midnight death squads, Mister Logan, funded by the right.

HAPPY: That's not our problem.

CORTEZ: This was your plan. Make me even more odious to the far right.

HAPPY: I don't play politics, Miss Cortez. I wouldn't dream of playing with your life.

CORTEZ: I can be either a martyr or an emigré. Thank you. Colombia, you have take away.

HAPPY: Denmark's a lovely place. Or New Zealand. I know a terrific travel agent. So many places to go, Miss Cortez. The world's at your feet.

CORTEZ: Stop conning me.

HAPPY: You're right. I am conning you. How low of me. *(Pause)* I apologize for the dysentery. As gentlemen, we tried to meet you halfway. Please believe this. Here, government is striving for some aspect of perfection. I came to accept your convictions. You've something which I envy.

CORTEZ: Pray tell, what?

HAPPY: Intellectual dedication.

CORTEZ: Am I to believe you?

HAPPY: Yes. Particularly because you're a sexual woman. I mean, the hot motor is working. I hear sizzling Latin rhythms. I hear love singing. You're a formidable individual, Miss Cortez. And I admire the roundness of your breasts. Your beautiful rosewater lips. Why should I be shy? Perhaps we could have dinner? *(Pause)* Tomorrow we take you to the airport.

CORTEZ: And you're going to miss me?

HAPPY: Yes.

CORTEZ: Isn't that a wedding ring?

HAPPY: It was.

CORTEZ: Who taught you the art of flirting, Mister Logan?

HAPPY: American instinct.

CORTEZ: I see. *(Pause)* Cultivate your chastity, Mister Logan. So when your princess comes, she'll be able to admire you. *(Silence)* Will there be a press conference at the airport?

HAPPY: No.

CORTEZ: And if I'm recognized at the airport by reporters?

HAPPY: You'll wear a disguise. A funny looking Stetson. A black veil. The best disguise is a subjective manner. Just be demure, Miss Cortez.

CORTEZ: And what has happened to Angelica?

HAPPY: She was released the day before.

CORTEZ: Did you molest her?

HAPPY: Did we molest you?

CORTEZ: She passed me a note, Mister Logan.

HAPPY: And did you pass her a note?

CORTEZ: She and I will remember this incident for a very long time. I will empty myself of it.

HAPPY: Be my guest.

CORTEZ: I will portray you.

HAPPY: How so?

CORTEZ: Emblematically. On all fours.

HAPPY: As you wish. Here's your travel prescription. *(Hands over pills for dysentery)* Won't you have dinner with me?

CORTEZ: How kind of you, Mister Logan. You show a side of civility so late in the day. Could it be that a gentleman hides inside? The ugly troll under the toll bridge. A political Rumpelstilskin. I came for a literary award but leave with the anger of a rape victim. Am I really more dangerous than you, Mister Logan?

HAPPY: Yes. Your language, Miss Cortez. It's your language.

CORTEZ: And if we had met at a bar, under different circumstances...

HAPPY: Are you making a pass at me, Miss Cortez?

CORTEZ: Of course. Can't you tell?

HAPPY: I understand your human needs. Perhaps a good man between your legs would vivify you?

CORTEZ: What a mature thing to say. You put love so delicately.

HAPPY: *(Falsely flattered)* Thank you.

CORTEZ: The inferior male hormones in your blood, Mister Logan, have set you back a thousand years. You need a shot of estrogen and a large dose of rationality. Shout your mother's name when you reach your final coronary. You have no savior. How I pity you.

Scene Eleven

(Day six. Lounge)

FULLER: He came in this morning without calling.

HAPPY: Where was I?

FULLER: I don't know. He went over the files. Checked the paper shredder. Asked a lot of questions.

HAPPY: What's his name?

FULLER: Monteith.

HAPPY: The Under-Secretary?

FULLER: Yes.

HAPPY: Did he say when he was coming back?

FULLER: No. Happy, he's a real snoop.

HAPPY: Did he visit the rooms?

FULLER: Yes. Ward B.

HAPPY: The Israeli's?

FULLER: Yes.

HAPPY: Why the hell didn't you detour him?

FULLER: He's a charging bull.

HAPPY: Shit, shit, shit. I've got to make a dozen phone calls. You really blew it, Fuller.

FULLER: Hell, Monteith's got top clearance.

HAPPY: Smarts, Fuller...this is the beginning of a set-up. Can't you smell it? Did he speak with the detainees?

FULLER: Yeah.

HAPPY: Someone blew the whistle on us.

FULLER: Why?

HAPPY: Because the wheel turns.

FULLER: Who?

HAPPY: An insider. Maybe a medic. Or food services. Shit. We should clean house now. These guys will stop at nothing. Countermanding the last eighteen months of bonuses. Just when we were rolling.

FULLER: Aguneir's bruises are outrageous, Happy.

HAPPY: Did he speak to Monteith?

FULLER: No.

HAPPY: Out he goes. Call the garage. Get a driver ready. And flight arrangements. Did Monteith take photos?

FULLER: Yes.

HAPPY: We're fucked! They're going to ream us! Of all times for an on-site. Shit, shit, shit! Give me the keys to Aguneir's room.

FULLER: The damage is done.

HAPPY: Give me the fucking keys.

FULLER: *(Tossing keys)* I thought you were on good terms with the brass.

HAPPY: So did I.

FULLER: Don't do anything rash, Happy.

HAPPY: They're looking for a scapegoat. Traffic light just changed color in Washington. This building was off limits to Congress. State was supposed to protect us. We have to cover our asses now. Such bastards at State. You'd think after cracking two headliners, they'd throw us a bone. I'm going to name Delancy and his teammates. Such fucking bastards in Washington. We can fix it. Enough belly aching. I'm getting rid of the Jew.

Scene Twelve

(Continuation as if MONTEITH *is already present. Lounge. Day six)*

MONTEITH: Are you Mister Logan?

HAPPY: Yes.

MONTEITH: Agent Fuller has discussed the events of the last two weeks with me. Is there anything you care to say with regard to his statement?

HAPPY: You issued a report, Fuller?

FULLER: *(Reluctantly)* No.

MONTEITH: Mister Logan, this is an informal investigation.

HAPPY: Don't railroad me with games about procedure.

MONTEITH: You've a bright set of brass balls, Mister Logan. Don't dismiss this gross irregularities here. And wipe that smirk off your face.

HAPPY: I'm not responsible for health problems within this building.

MONTEITH: I think you are. And your associate. Ward B's like a chamber of horrors.

HAPPY: You guys structured Ward B. We're just following established policy.

MONTEITH: I don't think so, Mister Logan.

HAPPY: Are you bringing us up for charges?

MONTEITH: *(Nonchalant)* I'm going to hang you out to dry, yes.

HAPPY: You knew he was a diabetic. *(Pause)* We had requests from your channels to detain him, to uncover his links with the terrorists in New York. I have letters saying so. And I can release these letters to the press.

(Pause) Think about it. I've no loyalty to Delancy and his team.

MONTEITH: Mister Logan, Chaim Aguneir is in critical condition. Ostensibly, from a massive stroke. The timing couldn't be worse. The lacerations to his face and upper chest are simply astounding. Don't ask me to believe this came from a fall in the shower. If either one of you induced this problem...well, the Devil has joined our little coterie at Immigration Services. If you lie to me, I promise to be double punitive. You can bet your pensions on that.

FULLER: We were working under extreme pressure, brought on by your people. You know our ways.

MONTEITH: I didn't come here to hand our citations for valor, Mister Fuller. Don't tell me dirty business was sanctioned by a Washington bureau. But if you reveal, to the best of your knowledge, who ordered the Israeli's beating and which of you complied with that order...it would make my visit that much simpler. Tell me who withheld his insulin...who extorted compliance from the medics with the insulin substitute...who assumed the freedom to play Almighty God, gentlemen. *(Pause)* If the Israeli comes out of his stroke, I can circumvent this interview. I'm a pessimist by nature. *(Pause)* Gentlemen, now's the time to sing. *(Pause)* The young woman Cortez is free to meet a death squad outside her home in Bogota. Stunning work, gentlemen.

FULLER: We were just following your office's line.

HAPPY: We never went to the press. You guys did.

MONTEITH: The momentum started here. Under your nose. You should have just sent the woman back on the next plane. Yes, gentlemen. So, no more snivelling. You can incriminate yourselves, or each other. I don't really care. Just don't waste my time.

HAPPY: Who sent you? *(Pause)* I would like advice from counsel, Mister Monteith.

MONTEITH: I'm sorry, Mister Logan, but we will carry on as though marooned far away from civilization. We can pretend behind closed doors. Tell each other stories. Perhaps strike a deal.

HAPPY: What sort of deal?

MONTEITH: A deal of mutual convenience.

FULLER: For whom?

MONTEITH: For our warm little family.

FULLER: *(After a beat)* Alright.

MONTEITH: Mister Logan?

HAPPY: I need to think it over.

MONTEITH: *(After a beat)* Mister Logan?

HAPPY: Alright.

MONTEITH: Mister Logan, were you assigned Chaim Aguneir?

HAPPY: What difference does it make? *(Pause)* I interceded with Aguneir's interrogation. Fuller had trouble.

MONTEITH: Mister Fuller, do you know if Mister Logan used excessive physical punishment during the interrogation?

FULLER: No.

MONTEITH: But you were aware of Chaim Aguneir's condition?

FULLER: Only what you yourself know.

MONTEITH: Is Mister Logan a sadist?

FULLER: I don't think so.

MONTEITH: Do you think we should employ sadists in this department?

HAPPY: Now just a second, damnit...

MONTEITH: *(Ignoring* HAPPY*)* Mister Fuller, on occasion the branches of government conflict with one another. Was your department issued a memorandum from another agency?

FULLER: Mister Logan receives all memorandums.

MONTEITH: Can you name someone above Mister Logan who may have issued any orders to play hard ball with a detainee? *(Silence)* Mister Logan, were there any memorandums about this?

HAPPY: Regarding Cortez from Colombia, yes.

MONTEITH: Can I see this memorandum?

HAPPY: Only telephone confirmation.

MONTEITH: Saying what?

HAPPY: You know the wording.

MONTEITH: Be explicit, Mister Logan, lest I risk a misunderstanding.

HAPPY: Mister Monteith, I'm not a rookie at this sort of thing. I like my department. Have pride in my work. Your questions are demoralizing.

MONTEITH: I'm very sorry, Mister Logan.

HAPPY: We do a very good job at Immigration.

MONTEITH: Yes, I know.

HAPPY: You send us lists of undesirables. You request intelligence information. We obey. It's a little hypocritical, Mister Monteith—sir—to expect us to play clean with your dirty favors. You're here because you need a fall guy. *(Pause)* I really wish I knew who sent you. It's a bit disheartening to feel like a political stooge. Don't I have intrinsic worth? It's true about

the Israeli. Orders were to detain him. To fucking
crack him. Quickly. There was danger in New York.
A shitload of bombings. His arrogance was too rich
for my blood, Mister Monteith. I found I hated things
about him. His demoniacal bullshit. I'm not a fucking
anti-Semite. We need Jews in the world. But it's very
hard to like an uppity Jew, like Chiam Aguneir. Arab
racist, pure and simple. Well, be glad that I cracked the
son-of-a-bitch. A menace to our society. It makes me
very happy to serve Immigration. *(Pause)* Of course,
you want to go about this with white gloves and an
angel's halo. We're not fucking pansies here, Mister
Monteith. We're patriotic, hard working family men
in a thankless role. Working in twilight so you pretty
boys can look good. So I advise you to return to your
particular branch up there in the fucking stratosphere
and convey my profound regrets over the Israeli's
untimely stroke. *(Pause)* And, should he drop dead in
the hospital, we can shed crocodile tears and consider
ourselves lucky for a time.

MONTEITH: For your sake, pray that he comes through.
Do you understand? I will take a life for a life.

FULLER: We will pray.

MONTEITH: Perhaps at this point I might do better
talking with you alone.

HAPPY: There's no need to. Fuller and I are very close.

MONTEITH: Mister Logan, would you excuse us...
please?

HAPPY: You're not going to play us against each other.
Don't waste your time. I won't say a word against
Fuller. He's like a brother. And he'll say the same.

MONTEITH: Mister Logan, I'll be with you shortly.
Please don't hold up this review.

HAPPY: Fuller, do we have a pact?

FULLER: Yeah.

HAPPY: You mean it.

FULLER: Yeah.

HAPPY: We're together forever?

FULLER: Yeah, Happy.

HAPPY: God bless you, Fuller. You're the man of the hour.

MONTEITH: Get lost, Mister Logan. I'll call you when I need you.

Scene Thirteen

(Day six continued)

MONTEITH: Mister Fuller, I'm about to tell you the fable of the fox and the cocker spaniel. *(Pause)* There was once a farm with the kindest family around. And on this wonderful farm were all sorts of livestock who lived very wonderful lives. They had sheep and cows and ducks and pigs and, of course, a hen house. The family kept the farm in order with their trusty cocker spaniel. Whenever there was any trouble, the cocker spaniel would bark and warn the family. One day, a fox snuck into the farm and passed itself off as one of the farm goats. Everyone was fooled but the cocker spaniel. The cocker spaniel had keen sense, Mister Fuller. *(Pause)* If you've heard this story before, I'll stop... *(Pause)* So the spaniel approached the fox one day and let him know that not everyone was fooled. But the fox was clever and spoke back: "Hey, I'm just like you...in need of a good home. I promise not to do any harm. Just treat me like one of the gang." *(Pause)* Now the spaniel felt in his bones that this was wrong, but just could not find the anger to bark at this tricky little fox. Then, some weeks later, the hens were

attacked by the fox. *(Pause)* Now the family rounded
up all the animals that day and asked them what they
knew. And you know what? The fox whispered to the
spaniel "Don't be pernicious". *(Pause)* Mister Fuller,
do you know the meaning of pernicious? *(Pause)* It
is sinful to be pernicious. Don't put the family in
peril...I want to talk to you about loyalty, Mister Fuller.
When I was in grad school, for pleasure I read Hegel.
You would benefit by his wisdom. You have ties
with friends and family. You have responsibility to
yourself. You have allegiance to the State. Whenever
there is a conflict with these three categories, Mister
Fuller, which do you choose? *(Pause)* Mister Fuller,
the irregularities and criminal proceedings in this
detention center astound one. I'm giving you a chance
to save your own neck. I must turn someone in. If I
must, all of you will be indicted. Make my case easier,
and you can keep your job. *(Pause)* Well, I'm going
to leave a pencil and legal pad for you to write a
deposition on your superior, Mister Logan. Be truthful
and merciless, Mister Fuller, because in this business
there are no loyalties.

Scene Fifteen

(Day Seven. Lounge)

MONTEITH: Sit down, Mister Logan. *(Pause)* Agent
Fuller's deposition was completed yesterday.

HAPPY: Is it consistent with mine?

MONTEITH: No.

HAPPY: Serious discrepancies?

MONTEITH: Yes.

HAPPY: What exactly did Fuller say?

MONTEITH: That you brutalized Chaim Aguneir with a rubber hose.

(HAPPY *tries to interrupt*)

MONTEITH: And that your attack contributed to his stroke.

HAPPY: It's not true.

MONTEITH: Mister Logan, it would help your case considerably if you changed your own statement. *(Pause)* Mister Logan, I understand you have a daughter.

HAPPY: Yes?

MONTEITH: How old is she?

HAPPY: Almost six.

MONTEITH: Do you love her?

HAPPY: Indeed I do.

MONTEITH: What is her name?

HAPPY: Ginger.

MONTEITH: Do you want good things for your little girl?

HAPPY: Of course.

MONTEITH: I have a little girl too. Her name is Suzy. She can steal your heart so tenderly. Daddy...Daddy... Daddy...look what fatherhood does to a man...*(Pause)* Mister Logan, why not speak the truth? We could close this investigation that much sooner. Do it for Ginger. *(Pause)* I look at your face, Mister Logan, and my heart goes out to you. I see guilt, contortion, sorrow. Such a dreadful sight. I see tremendous sickness and pain in your leathered face. Make a full admission. Clear your conscience. How will you ever find peace in your present state? *(Pause)* Cigarette? Coffee? *(Pause)* Mister Logan...I want to tell you about the extraordinary fable of the errant church mouse and the sacred wine cellar. Yes, there in the hidden chambers of a lovely country church, lived a meek and lonely church mouse. The church mouse cooked and cleaned and was generally an upstanding inhabitant of the church community. But it came to pass that the church mouse discovered the sacred wine of old in the church cellar. At first the mouse refused to open the wine. But, after a time, the mouse-with some cheek-began to use teaspoons of wine for cooking. And regrettably, the mouse began to drink directly from the wine bottles. His deviant behavior eventually gave him away. Slurred speech, aggressive, a little red nose. A drunk is a drunk. *(Pause)* Have you heard this story, Mister Logan? It's a very old story. *(Pause)* The community recognized his sickness and his unmitigated sadness. He was after all a disgusting alcoholic church mouse. Prematurely wizened. So hideous to the community. He would receive his just punishment. For secretly, the mouse yearned for his vindication. For secretly, we all yearn for vindication. How many bridges must we cross, Mister Logan? I see your pockmarked skin turning color. Release yourself. I promise not to abuse you. Say how you picked up the weapon, and how many times you struck the Israeli. Tell me what was in your tormented mind during the attack. All I ask is for details. Mister Logan, was it better than any activity in bed? *(Pause)* Mister Logan, pick up the pencil and write. The community will support you. You are a wounded bird in need of a milk tit. A new world awaits you. *(After a pause)* Your friend can rest easy now that you will come to his aid. I want you to tell him that. He'll be here shortly. It will be your honesty, Mister Logan, which will impress him the most. And your new found grace. May you find a bit of peace in your heart. Write.

HAPPY: *(Slowly picking up pencil. Unable to write)* And how is Aguneir?

MONTEITH: He died this morning.

HAPPY: Then whatever I write won't matter. You have Fuller's testimony.

MONTEITH: *(Fatherly)* Put it down on paper, Mister Logan. Word for word. It will be for your benefit alone. *(Exits)*

HAPPY: *(To MONTEITH's chair)* Pride makes me vain. Love has deserted me. And this unsightly twist in my glorious career, at the worst possible time...who cursed me? I love my country. I so do love my country. Aguneir, I have made countless sacrifices to my beloved country. My country means everything to me. Like all the stars in the sky. Dear God in Heaven, give me back my country.

Scene Sixteen

(Later, Day Seven. Lounge)

HAPPY: Talk to me.

FULLER: What should I say? *(Pause)* You don't look good.

HAPPY: When your car broke down last summer, who gave you a loaner?

FULLER: You did.

HAPPY: Because I care. I'm built that way. And who helped you with the bank loan for that hernia operation?

FULLER: You did.

HAPPY: I'm not a bad guy, as guys go, eh Fuller? With my friends, I go deep. You understand that. You pain is my pain. I don't want to see you in pain. You deserve better. I deserve better. Isn't that so? *(Pause)* Look at me, Fuller. I feel a little broken inside. *(Pause)* Why the fuck did you capitulate?

FULLER: I only told the truth.

HAPPY: Fuller...

FULLER: They're coming down hard, Happy. These guys are heavyweights.

HAPPY: Monteith dances on your toes and you go down. I know why. I know why. Your wife. You talked to your wife. Tell me you talked with your wife.

FULLER: I talked with my wife.

HAPPY: And she cried.

FULLER: Yeah.

HAPPY: And she talked you into giving testimony, because she didn't want to see you in prison.

FULLER: That's right.

HAPPY: And because I don't figure in with your situation, I'm just a piece of shit.

FULLER: No.

HAPPY: You're always being pulled by someone's strings. You realize this.

FULLER: We're all going through the same fucking ringer. *(Traded silences)* Yeah.

HAPPY: Yeah?

FULLER: I've family to worry over. I got responsibilities, Happy. I need to survive. Can't do time in jail. My ass is on the line. I didn't cause this shit. Didn't beat the Jew. My nose is clean. I got to tell the truth. I got to.

HAPPY: I thought we had a pact. Didn't we have a goddamn pact? Tell me we didn't have a goddamn pact.

FULLER: I need to stay clean, Happy.

HAPPY: Clean?

FULLER: Monteith says you've a record for past abuse. I didn't know you were on probation.

HAPPY: You made a deal, didn't you, Fuller?

FULLER: No, Happy.

HAPPY: Don't bullshit me. Tell me you made a deal.

FULLER: No deal.

HAPPY: They're going to put me away for a long long time, Fuller. Twenty years. You think I'm fooling? I'm expendable. Don't even cost a fucking nickle. I'm an example for the department. They're showing the press they can clean house. Is that fair, Fuller?

FULLER: No.

HAPPY: Don't patronize me, Fuller. I was your friend. *(Pause)* You got to show solidarity now. I'm running out of time. *(Pause)* Monteith showed me your deposition. You gave away the candy store.

FULLER: It was given under duress.

HAPPY: Let me tell you about duress. I'm in duress. You understand that? We're members of the same fraternity. A union of average American guys. Of tobacco and booze, the great late night bouts at the corner tavern. We're a fellowship, Fuller. There are unspoken covenants. Don't break a sacred covenant. Turning me over like white trash won't do. Don't play the black scarecrow. We're joined at the hip, man. You go nowhere without me. I go down, you go down. You get orders from me. We're still brethren.

FULLER: Aguneir's dead.

HAPPY: I know.

FULLER: What do you want me to do?

HAPPY: Meet with my attorney.

FULLER: To what purpose?

HAPPY: He has a scheme.

FULLER: Come on, Happy. They got us cornered. They have my deposition.

HAPPY: You can countermand it.

FULLER: No.

HAPPY: Shit.

FULLER: Hey...

HAPPY: Hey, weasel.

FULLER: My attorney put me under wraps.

HAPPY: We've got to talk, Fuller. There's no other way. Put out for me. Listen to me. Come downstairs. Right now. I'll buy you lunch. My guy's at the restaurant waiting. Talk to him for one hour. One fucking hour. No pressure. I promise. We're going to walk out free men.

FULLER: Happy, what's the use?

HAPPY: There's an angle. My lawyer's got an angle. Just come with me, damnit. We can fight this with an appeal. We'll go after them. This thing can be fought. But I can't do it alone. Do you understand, Fuller. I can't do it alone.

FULLER: I was promised immunity.

HAPPY: You got immunity?

FULLER: Yeah.

HAPPY: You fucking scumbag.

FULLER: They forced it on me.

HAPPY: Look what's going down. Look. Look. Shit.
Hey, Fuller...you know...look, friend...don't shit me...
Fuller, come with me right now...

FULLER: I can't.

HAPPY: You got to help me, 'cause no one else can.
I'll buy you lunch. Come on. Fuller... *(Pause)* Look
sweetheart, I'm running out of time. My lawyer's going
to fix everything. For you and for me. Our friendship's
at stake and I'm getting angry and nasty and so
fucking upset, like I'm getting an ulcer right now
waiting each minute you dick around here, like I don't
enjoy getting the shaft from my friend, my colleague,
my subordinate, like it's time to join the goddamn rank
and file, you and me, tight and proud, like don't play
Judas Asshole, you little son-of-a-bitch, 'cause you
know all hell will break loose on you before you can
say purple Uncle Remus.

FULLER: Happy, you need more help than I can give.

HAPPY: Damnit, save my ass!

FULLER: I've tried.

HAPPY: Fuller...read my lips...I'll kill you, if you fuck
me up. I swear to God. I'll kill you. Don't walk away
from me. Don't play moral high road shit. Just come
with me. Just get in the fucking elevator and eat your
goddamn tuna salad with my lawyer downstairs.
Understand? Get your hat and coat and come with
me to the elevator. Capice? *(Pause)* Fuller, my blood's
boiling and I'm about to burst. I'll count to three.
Slowly. With all the fucking dignity I can muster.
(Pause) One. Two. Three. *(Silence)* Fuller, I'm going
to count once more. Out of respect to your dear wife.
(Pause) One. Two.

(HAPPY slugs FULLER in face. FULLER hits the floor)

HAPPY: Get up, Fuller, and get your silly hat and coat.
Don't waste a second of my precious time.

Scene Seventeen

(Day Eight. Lounge—Dimly lit)

HAPPY: I left the pizza in the oven, because I couldn't
stand being in the house alone. Her car was still in the
driveway. I waited. She came out with Ginger. They
drove away after they caught a glimpse of me. *(Pause)*
No note. No explanation. Nothing. *(Pause)* I went up
to the bedroom and packed all my things. Took them
outside on the front lawn. Bawled like a baby. Poured
gasoline. Lit it. Blazed like a great inferno. Billows of
smoke. Spirits in the sky. Neighbors ran out to watch.
I went back inside to get the drapes off the windows.
Poured gasoline. Lit it. *(Pause)* I burned my wallet
and my shoes and every family photograph. *(Pause)*
Went back inside. Smoke was pushing out of the
oven. Phoned the authorities. Forgot my address. Got
in the car. Knocked over the garbage cans. Drove to
the highway. Went back over a dozen years. Saw my
wife's first car. The Plymouth. By the shoulder of the
road. Her high hemline of her skirt. Her legs. Her flat
tire. Her voice. I jacked up her car. Asked her to dinner.
Asked her to marry me. I fixed her tire. *(Pause)* When
Ginger was born, we knew we were in love. *(Pause)* I
drove to the pawn shop, with her shitty silverware and
the Sony Trinitron. It was a place where no permit is
necessary. I already had bullets. I bought a sandwich. I
loaded the gun. *(Pause)* I waited for Joyce to return.

Scene Eighteen

(Day Nine. CORTEZ's *room)*

FULLER: Any further questions?

CORTEZ: No.

FULLER: I've spoken to your colleagues at Harvard and they're to receive you in a private ceremony. A solution, we think. I gather you will leave the country after the trip to the college. Is there any other country in South America where you feel safe?

CORTEZ: I was thinking of France.

FULLER: Let me arrange a review board to assist you. I've completed your report. We appreciate your cooperation.

CORTEZ: *(After a silence)* I have compromised myself.

FULLER: Hardly.

CORTEZ: I did. There are things I cannot stand. I must push on. I'll have to pay for this later.

FULLER: You were undermined, Miss Cortez. We acted unfairly.

CORTEZ: You're quite different from Logan.

FULLER: It's the nature of a man's diet. A man's moral center. A man needs good influences. Like you, I have compromised myself. We are similar. I like your writing, Miss Cortez. You champion a good cause, in your own way. Your prose is vigorous, challenging, on target. Poor people need you. With the sweep of the Reagan years, you scare many flag wavers. Well, now you're free. Our borders are open. Enjoy New York. I apologize for the various hardships and misunderstandings incurred here. Your papers and visa are on the table. *(Pause)* Miss Cortez?

CORTEZ: *(Collecting her papers)* Neither you nor I are invincible. We find comfort in our respective pragmatism.

FULLER: Do we? *(Pause)* It's important to be realistic in the world we inhabit.

CORTEZ: Where is Mister Logan?

FULLER: Why do you ask?

CORTEZ: I've something to tell him.

FULLER: I'm afraid that will have to wait.

CORTEZ: Why?

FULLER: This morning Mister Logan shot himself with a revolver to his temple.

END OF PLAY

www.ingramcontent.com/pod-product-compliance
Lightning Source LLC
Chambersburg PA
CBHW052222090426
42741CB00010B/2647